982.14
G

ME AND MY GIRL

Vocal selections

Produced by
RICHARD ARMITAGE, TERRY ALLEN KRAMER
JAMES M. NEDERLANDER and
STAGE PROMOTIONS LIMITED & CO.

Starring
ROBERT LINDSAY
MARYANN PLUNKETT
GEORGE S. IRVING

Featuring
JANE CONNELL
JANE SUMMERHAYS

Directed by
MIKE OCKRENT

Score by
NOEL GAY

Book and Lyrics by
L. ARTHUR ROSE and
DOUGLAS FURBER

Photos by
ALAN BERLINER

ISBN 0-88188-538-X

HL Hal Leonard Publishing Corporation
7777 West Bluemound Road P.O. Box 13819 Milwaukee, WI 53213

Applications for performance of this work, whether legitimate,
stock, amateur, or foreign, should be addressed to:
NOEL GAY MUSIC CO. LTD.
24 Denmark Street
London WC2H
8NJ England

Robert Lindsay   Maryann Plunkett

Maryann Plunkett   Robert Lindsay

Jane Summerhays   Robert Lindsay

Robert Lindsay   Jane Summerhays

Robert Lindsay   George S. Irving

Jane Connell   *George S. Irving*

THINKING OF NO ONE BUT ME

Words by DOUGLAS FURBER
Music by NOEL GAY

mon - ey can buy_____ I'll make my lim - it the

sky_____ This is "Hoo - ray and good- bye"_____

_____ While I'm young and health - y, I'll

find some - one wealth - y, {Some rich ci - ty / Some big ci - ty}

ME AND MY GIRL

Words by DOUGLAS FURBER
Music by NOEL GAY

HOLD MY HAND

Words by HARRY GRAHAM
Music by MAURICE ELWIN and NOEL GAY

Lyrics:
You re-quire a lot of look-ing af-ter;

That's one job in which I take a pride.

(She)You can al-ways make me smile, make my jour-ney seem worth-while.

ONCE YOU LOSE YOUR HEART

Words and Music by
NOEL GAY

LAMBETH WALK

Words by DOUGLAS FURBER
Music by NOEL GAY

THE SUN HAS GOT HIS HAT ON
(HE'S COMING OUT TODAY)

Words and Music by RALPH BUTLER
and NOEL GAY

TAKE IT ON THE CHIN

Words and Music by Noel Gay
and Douglas Furber

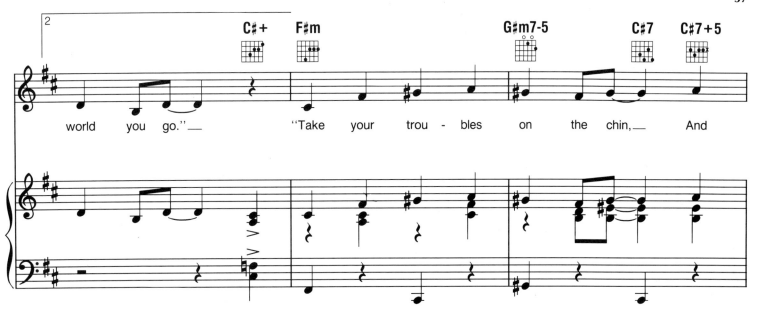

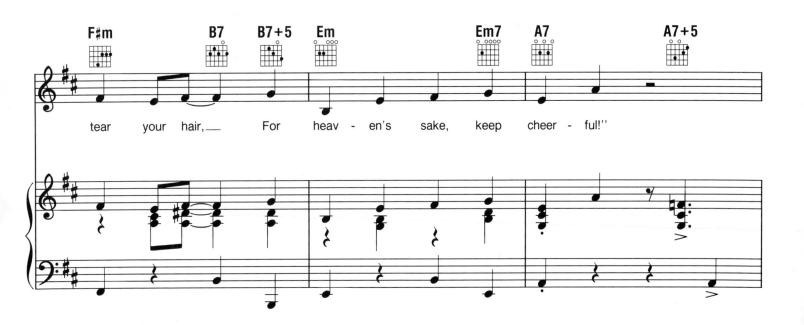

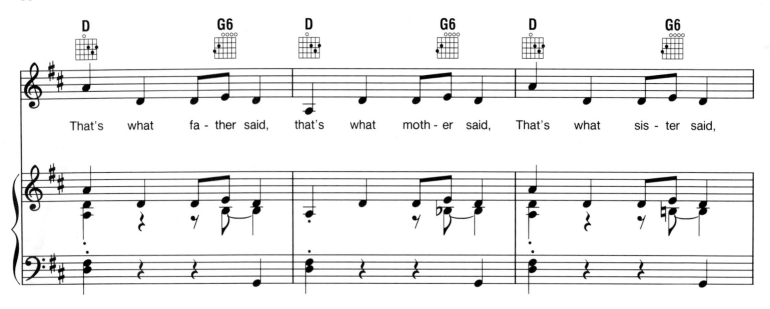

That's what fa-ther said, that's what moth-er said, That's what sis-ter said,

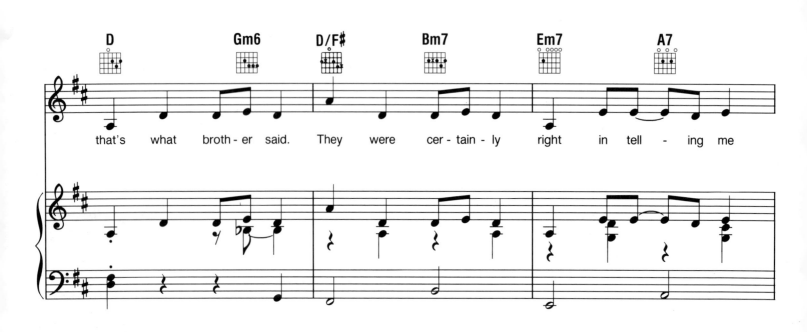

that's what broth-er said. They were cer-tain-ly right in tell - ing me

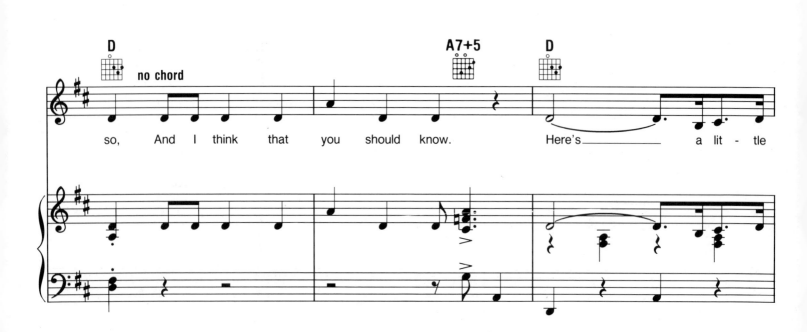

so, And I think that you should know. Here's_____ a lit - tle

LOVE MAKES THE WORLD GO ROUND

Words and Music by
NOEL GAY

46

LEANING ON A LAMP-POST

Moderately, with a lilting swing

Words and Music by
NOEL GAY

Lean - ing on a lamp, May-be you think I look a tramp, Or you may

think I'm hang-ing 'round to steal a car. _____ But

no, I'm not a crook, And if you think that's what I look, I'll tell you

never leave me flat, She's not a girl like that, She's ab-so-lute-ly won-der-ful and mar-ve-lous and beau-ti-ful, And an-y-one can un-der-stand why I'm lean-ing on a lamp-post at the cor-ner of the street, In case a cer-tain lit-tle la-dy comes by. I'm

YOU WOULD IF YOU COULD

Words and Music by NOEL GAY
and DOUGLAS FURBER